C000165332

Anxious Times

The Bible Reading Fellowship
15 The Chambers, Vineyard
Abingdon OX14 3FE
brf.org.uk

The Bible Reading Fellowship (BRF) is a Registered Charity (233280)

ISBN 978 0 85746 660 0
First published 2018
10 9 8 7 6 5 4 3 2 1 0
All rights reserved

Acknowledgements
Scripture quotations from The Holy Bible, New International Version (Anglicised edition) copyright
© 1979, 1984, 2011 by Biblica. Used by permission of Hodder & Stoughton Publishers, a Hachette UK
company. All rights reserved. 'NIV' is a registered trademark of Biblica. UK trademark number 1448790.

Every effort has been made to trace and contact copyright owners for material used in this resource. We
apologise for any inadvertent omissions or errors, and would ask those concerned to contact us so that
full acknowledgement can be made in the future.

A catalogue record for this book is available from the British Library

Printed and bound by The Graphic Design House

Anxious Times

Carmel Thomason

Foreword

Archbishop John Sentamu

This book is to be savoured, not rushed. As an antidote to anxiety, it will repay a measured reading, just one short chapter a day.

A friend sent me a card last Christmas, with the greeting, 'I hope you are well. The world isn't.' That encapsulated what many people are feeling. Asked if he was worried about the possibility of nuclear war, Pope Francis said recently, 'I think we are at the very limit. I am really afraid of this. One accident is enough to precipitate things.'

Quite apart from our daily diet of gloomy news, there's also an unidentified uncertainty hanging in the air. The old signposts which pointed the way to faith and hope have been defaced, and frustrated hope is audible, visible and smellable. Despair is polluting our air. We are more and more reliant on inner resources to tackle the general foreboding. This book will help to replenish them.

The Bible has much to say about worry and fear, and how to cope with them. Unlike some overenthusiastic preachers, it doesn't chastise us or pump us up with spiritual steroids which insist the world will end any minute now, so there's nothing to worry about. Jesus readily acknowledged the unease that we all feel from time to time and engaged in a bit of leg-pulling to help us get through it:

> 'Look at the birds of the air; they do not sow or reap or store away in barns, and yet your heavenly Father feeds them. Are you not much more valuable than they? Can any one of you by worrying add a single hour to your life?'
> MATTHEW 6:26–27

It is very good news that BRF recognises the need to publish some gentle and realistic Christian advice about a 21st-century virus and that Carmel Thomason has written it.

Introduction

'Peace I leave with you; my peace I give you. I do not give to you as the world gives. Do not let your hearts be troubled and do not be afraid.'
JOHN 14:27

As I write this, in August 2017, by many indices the world is safer than at any other time in human history. At the same time many people are living more afraid than ever before. Across Europe this year the terrorist threat has fluctuated between severe, meaning an attack is highly likely, and critical, meaning an attack is expected imminently. Everyday modes of transport are being used as weapons, and yet terrorist experts tell us we are more likely to be struck by lightning than by a terrorist's bullet.

On first hearing that comparison, I thought, 'I don't know anyone who has been struck by lightning.' The next day I read a news story about people injured by lightning strikes in France.

I don't find these types of statistics helpful. Telling me there is a greater danger from something I never considered dangerous just gives me one more thing to worry about. Rather than putting my fear into perspective, it reinforces an underlying anxiety that the world is a dangerous place. It's like saying, 'What's the worst that could happen?' Do you want to ask another question, because I've got a good imagination?

Research has shown that some chronic worriers use their worry to suppress and avoid difficult emotions, protecting themselves from the impact of living and the raw feelings that can come with it. Paradoxically, in attempting to protect ourselves from feeling fear, it seems by worrying we may be making ourselves more anxious and afraid.

We all know that telling someone not to be afraid doesn't stop them feeling afraid. We can't think our way out of fear, and for all our 21st-century technological advances, we still can't control every aspect of life.

There are some things, such as giant sinkholes in the road, that are clearly unsafe, but for the most part life isn't divided so easily into safe and unsafe. Despite this, there is a tendency to want to label everything, to sort it into categories we can recognise, even if we can't understand them. There is a sense of certainty in doing that, but it can also lead to an uncomfortable 'them and us' way of looking at the world, a dualistic, divisive way of thinking.

Even if we try to keep the unknown at arm's length, it doesn't guarantee safety. Sometimes even people close to us will let us down. Jesus was betrayed by a close friend, Judas, one of his chosen disciples. We could use that evidence to say we can't trust anyone; or we could say that Jesus had twelve disciples, so if we're weighing up risk, there's a much better chance of finding love than betrayal.

Being open to love doesn't mean being naive. We'd probably all agree it's not a good idea to walk down the street with cash hanging out of your back pocket, but there is a world of difference between living aware and retreating to a fortress. Through experience we can become cynical or we can become wise. Someone once said to me, 'In life, there's your stuff, other people's stuff and God's stuff. Don't try to carry what's not yours.' Letting go and accepting uncertainty have been huge lessons for me, and ones I continue to learn.

We like to think our anxieties are somehow different, special or more acute than those of previous generations. If that were true, why did Jesus preach so often about worry and anxiety?

Jesus' resurrection demonstrates a power that casts out fear, even of death. Unfortunately, sometimes as Christians we take Jesus' message not to be afraid and isolate it from other scriptural teachings that demonstrate practical ways to control our worry and live with confidence – ways that are only now being evidenced through science as effective in controlling anxiety.

I've come to believe that feeling afraid and being afraid are different. The week after the 9/11 terror attack in New York I travelled to the USA on a flight with rows and rows of empty seats. I was nervous about going, a fear exacerbated on my return flight when the plane's computers failed and the captain's voice came over the tannoy telling us it wasn't safe to proceed over the Atlantic so we were being diverted to New York. There will always be circumstances that cause us to feel afraid, but this doesn't need to hold us back from living our lives fully in the way that avoidance of 'being afraid' so often does.

When I was asked to write this book, it was as a response to a collective anxiety about the current global situation. I'll admit, my first thought on receiving the request was an anxious one – how can I do this? After sitting with it for a while, I've done what I've learned to do when facing anything new or uncertain: I prayed, put my trust in God and did the best I could. I've shared scriptures that have supported me during times when I've felt anxious and worried. I've also shared experiences that have helped me in practical ways to let go of worry, accept living with uncertainty, trust in God and live with hope.

If you've picked up this book, it's likely either you or someone you know is struggling with anxiety. My prayer is that something within these pages will resonate with you and give you genuine hope that you won't always feel this way. A wise friend who was a prisoner of war during World War II once told me:

> Peace within a person is where it all starts. It is a peace that can't be disturbed or broken by outside events. I do hope that you will strive for that inner peace, however you find it. The actions of nations are merely the actions of men writ large and there are fewer of us left who were there to remind you of the depths to which a country can sink when hatred is allowed to fester.

As individuals, we may not be able to change the world, but we can change how we respond to the world. I pray that one by one we begin to break down the global barriers that divide us, by living with open, peaceful and fearless hearts.

Comfort in the word

About three in the afternoon Jesus cried out in a loud voice, '*Eli, Eli, lema sabachthani*?' (which means 'My God, my God, why have you forsaken me?').

On the wall of a small cellar in Cologne is scratched an anonymous three-line poem:

I believe in the sun, even when it is not shining.
I believe in love, even when I feel it not.
I believe in God, even when he is silent.

The words were found in a place where Jewish people hid during the Holocaust. It's hard to imagine a more fearful time or more fearful circumstances.

In times of fear it's a natural reaction to cry out, 'Where are you, God? Where are you in all this mess?' Yet sometimes as Christians we are made to feel as if our faith is failing if we question God's silence.

At times like these we can take our fears to Jesus and know he understands. Jesus knew God's silence. Never did anyone seem more alone than Jesus on the cross. Yet if we look to Psalm 22:1 we see his 'forsaken' cry echoes the words of David. In his time of greatest distress, Jesus uses words of scripture as a prayer and turns his cry of distress to one of faith. Jesus is not alone – God is with him in his word.

When anxious and under great stress, often we can struggle to find the words to express our feelings adequately. For thousands of years, men and women in similar situations have held on to words of scripture for support in times of need. There is something grounding and calming in that knowledge. God's word roots us in his love and reminds us we are not alone.

Lord, your word provides comfort in times of distress. Help me to recognise, even in my darkest hours, I am not alone.

Strength to carry on

'Father, if you are willing, take this cup from me; yet not my will, but yours be done.' An angel from heaven appeared to him and strengthened him. And being in anguish, he prayed more earnestly, and his sweat was like drops of blood falling to the ground.

Idly gazing out of the window, I saw a cat pounce on an unsuspecting sparrow. I knocked on the glass but the cat ignored me, pushing the bird from one paw to the other, like a small ball. I rushed to the door shouting, 'Leave it alone!' and the cat fled, leaving the sparrow on the ground. Now it was free, I thought the bird would fly away, but it didn't move.

Getting closer, I couldn't see any injuries but noticed the sparrow trembling, as if in shock. I don't know why its fear surprised me, but it did. I'd expected with the danger gone it would be on its way. Instead, the sparrow stayed rooted to the spot for at least ten minutes, until other birds came close by and it found the courage to spread its wings again.

Waiting for the sparrow to fly felt like an age. It got me thinking. How long have I allowed a fearful experience to keep me from living fully – minutes, hours, days, weeks, months, years perhaps?

When under threat of any kind, real or imagined, it is natural to experience fear as an unconscious, physical response. As uncomfortable as it is, no living being can escape this sensation.

If there is a scale of fear, in this scripture we see Jesus, sweating blood, at the limits of it. His faith is not shown by his lack of fear, but in his prayer of trust, through which he gains the strength to carry on in the face of that fear.

Lord, your cross led to resurrection. Guide me through my fear, trusting you have a higher purpose for my life.

MATTHEW 8:24–25

A constant calm

Suddenly a furious storm came up on the lake, so that the waves swept over the boat. But Jesus was sleeping. The disciples went and woke him, saying, 'Lord, save us! We're going to drown!'

A lifeboat volunteer once told me that going to sea in a gale feels like being in a washing machine on spin. No wonder the disciples are terrified. They follow Jesus on to the boat, probably imagining they are in for a relaxing sail, only to find the demands of discipleship are rarely smooth.

Without warning the weather changes, and the disciples find themselves at the centre of a fierce storm, with waves so high they cover the boat. Meanwhile, despite the commotion, Jesus sleeps. How can anyone sleep through that? Does he not realise what's happening to his friends? Does he not realise or care that they are about to drown?

'Wake up and save us!' Have you ever felt like Jesus was sleeping in your life? Have you ever felt like you are drowning under the weight of life's problems? Do you sometimes wait until you are panic-stricken before you ask for God's help?

Jesus asks, 'Why are you so afraid?' (Matthew 8:26). Then he stands up, rebukes the wind and the waves and all is calm.

Why were the disciples so afraid? Why are we so afraid? Do we imagine God works in emergencies, but falls asleep at all other times?

While we struggle through in our own strength, Jesus is a constant, waiting for us to call on him. He is the still eye of the storm, calm even when all around turns to chaos. We can always turn to Jesus for guidance, so why do we often leave it until we feel like we're drowning before reaching out for his support?

Lord, you are a calm presence in life's storms. In these rough seas, I reach out for your peace.

Choose to love

'You will hear of wars and rumours of wars, but see to it that you are not alarmed. Such things must happen, but the end is still to come.'

I grew up in the 1980s under the pervasive threat of nuclear war. As I write this, headlines tell me that North Korea's nuclear threat is real and terrifying. There's also news of toxic eggs, contaminated with the insecticide fipronil. When I was a teenager, eggs were at the centre of another safety crisis – the salmonella scare. Today news comes with a daily dose of déjà vu, and I begin to understand why Jesus says, 'see to it that you are not alarmed'. The dangers may change, but there are always dangers. I can't always control my exposure to these risks, but if I don't control my reaction to them I could live my whole life in fear.

Behind each news story are real people whose lives have changed beyond all recognition. I wouldn't like to see a day when I am unmoved by their suffering. The question is, moved to what?

In my home city, a 22-year-old man detonated a bomb after a pop concert at Manchester Arena, killing 23 people, including himself. Suddenly, the so-called war on terror felt very close. One of those killed was Olivia Campbell, 15. Following her death, Olivia's family issued a statement urging people, 'Please don't hate in Olivia's name; we choose to love.'

It's hard to be open to love when your heart is protecting itself in a fortress of anxiety. Not being alarmed is not the same as hiding from reality. It's creating space for compassion by focusing your energy on practical support, and holding the people affected, including those who cause pain, in your prayers. It's recognising danger in the world and still choosing to love and live with hope.

Lord, I trust you have put me in this time and place for a reason. Fill me with your peace, and give me the strength to always choose love and live with hope.

Beside me, always

'Be strong and courageous. Do not be afraid; do not be discouraged, for the Lord your God will be with you wherever you go.'

Courage, like forgiveness, is easy to talk about in the abstract but when we witness it lived out its impact can be life-changing. That's why people like the late Nelson Mandela are so admired throughout the world. In standing against apartheid and later leading reconciliation efforts in South Africa, Mandela wasn't simply talking the Christian message; he was living it.

We expect our leaders to be courageous, but this raises problems if we begin to think courage and forgiveness are the traits of special people. The corollary of that is we can believe there are things other people can do because they are not like us and don't feel fear.

It's natural to feel some level of anxiety when doing something for the first time. There's bound to be an element of stress when stepping into uncharted territory, unsure of what to expect and unable to prepare for what is coming next. Courage doesn't come from being fearless; it comes when we carry on despite our fears.

In the scriptures, God encourages all his people – weak and strong. Joshua is Moses' successor and a heroic figure, who leads the Israelites to the promised land and rest from war. Yet he too needed God's support and encouragement to face his fears, to be reminded that God was always by his side.

We all have unrestricted access to God. We should gain confidence and courage from knowing that he loves us and is encouraging us every step of the way.

Lord, sometimes I hold back from life because I am afraid. Help me feel the courage of your Spirit, knowing that whatever situation I may face, I am never alone, because you are beside me, always.

God knows your heart

'The eternal God is your refuge, and underneath are the everlasting arms.'

When my nephew was two years old, I took him to see *Aladdin* on stage. It was the first time he'd been to a theatre and his eyes widened as he took in the experience. There were bright colours, flashing lights, music and lots of people laughing, shouting and cheering. There was also a pantomime villain, Abanazer.

As we get older, booing and hissing at the baddie becomes part of the fun. It's easy to forget that for a young child immersed in the story, the threat of this villain can be real and terrifying. During the scenes with Abanazer, my nephew clung to me for safety. Then, as his fear subsided, his grip loosened. Watching the other children he summoned the courage to shout towards the stage at the top of his lungs, 'It's behind you!' There were more scary moments when he snuggled in for safety, but there were other joyous times when he danced and sang freely. It was a thrilling adventure for a little one, and when Aladdin finally thwarted Abanazer's evil plans my nephew celebrated wholeheartedly, throwing his arms in the air cheering, 'Yeah! We did it!'

As children, when we were scared, a hug from a parent or loved one was often all we needed to give us the courage to face the world again. As adults, we don't stop being scared, but often mask our fears with addictions – drink, drugs, medication, food, work, sex.

You don't need to put on a brave face with God. He knows your heart and he knows when you're scared. You don't need to explain yourself or pretend it's okay. Take refuge in his everlasting arms, feel his love and gain the strength to face your baddies, until you too can shout unreservedly, 'Yeah, Lord, we did it!'

Lord, even when I hide my fear from others you know what is troubling me and understand. Hold me close to you and strengthen me with your love.

Luke 10:41

Wake up

'Martha, Martha,' the Lord answered, 'you are worried and upset about many things.'

We use many words to mask fear, 'stress' being one of them. Stress has become the scourge of 21st-century life, affecting how we interact with other people and negatively impacting our health.

There are going to be times when our lives don't feel like our own, such as when we welcome a new baby, take on a new job or someone close to us is critically ill. However, such situations are not the cause of many people's chronic state of busyness and stress. Instead, what wears us down are the little things, such as always being the one to do the household chores, to taxi the children around, to do the church watch, to stay late at work, to organise the Christmas party, to run the errands no one else wants to do.

We've all been there, which is why it is so easy to empathise with Martha in this story. The weight of the world is on her shoulders. She is working hard in the kitchen, preparing the food for everyone, while her sister enjoys herself, listening to Jesus. It is a lesson to us all – the Saviour of the world is standing right in front of her, and Martha is too distracted with the routine busyness of life, preparing the house and the meal, to appreciate his company. Looking after Jesus has become another of her chores.

That's what happens when we worry constantly about being good enough. We create unnecessary responsibility and lose sight of our real priorities, until life itself becomes a chore. Don't allow yourself to be worn down worrying about everything and everyone. Let Jesus be your wake-up call. He accepts you as you are. Take time to listen to him, and recognise the best of life in front of you, right now.

Lord, sometimes there's so much to do; life feels overwhelming. Help me to recognise what is important and to prioritise, so I don't lose sight of your many blessings in my life.

A day at a time

'Therefore do not worry about tomorrow, for tomorrow will worry about itself. Each day has enough trouble of its own.'

For me, writing a book was a great lesson in patience, because it isn't something you can do in one sitting. Knowing I could be at the computer all day and all night and still have more to do forced me to write a little at a time, until gradually what at first seemed to be an overwhelming task was almost complete.

It sounds straightforward, but getting to that stage was far from easy. I'd spent years thinking I needed long periods of dedicated time to write something of length. In other words, I was waiting for the perfect circumstances to show up.

A successful writer told me, 'If you want to write, stop talking about it and just do it.' I remember bristling at the advice and thinking, 'She doesn't understand everything I've got to do.' I now see she was right. Instead of worrying about how I was going to do it and getting overwhelmed by an imagined future, or the size of the task, I needed to focus on what I could do on any one day.

Is there something you are putting off because you are waiting for the right circumstances, because the task feels too big, or because you're looking to the future and can't predict every step?

Jesus gives us a straightforward philosophy for life when he encourages us to take it one day at a time. There's a constancy in that, like putting one foot in front of the other, moving forward in faith and trusting God to light the parts of the path we can't yet see.

Lord, you promised to take care of me one day at a time. Help me focus on what I can do today, trusting you will guide my next step when the time comes.

MATTHEW 16:21–23

Strong words

> From that time on Jesus began to explain to his disciples that he must go to Jerusalem and suffer many things at the hands of the elders, the chief priests and the teachers of the law, and that he must be killed and on the third day be raised to life. Peter took him aside and began to rebuke him. 'Never, Lord!' he said. 'This shall never happen to you!' Jesus turned and said to Peter, 'Get behind me, Satan! You are a stumbling-block to me; you do not have in mind the concerns of God, but merely human concerns.'

'Get behind me, Satan!' What strong words. When temptations come or doubts set in, threatening to take us from God's purpose, it can be helpful to push such thoughts aside with a firm rebuke, as Jesus does here.

I can empathise with Peter. It's hard to accept God's plan might involve suffering of any kind, and it is not surprising Peter is so shocked at hearing the word 'killed' he doesn't take in the crucial 'raised to life' part that comes after. In response, Jesus' words are strong, but he explains his reaction with clarity.

Years ago, I confided in a Christian friend about feeling anxious, to which he said, 'That's the devil.' His response stunned me into silence. Was he saying I had the devil inside me or that my feelings were evil? My friend didn't mean to hurt me, but he did, by falling into the use of unhelpful religious jargon, where any uncomfortable emotion is labelled 'the devil'.

Looking back, I like to think that my friend meant fear and anxiety were keeping me from experiencing God's best for my life, but I wonder how many people have turned away from churches through anxious misunderstandings, when good-hearted people have rushed to speak Jesus' words without first pausing to seek his wisdom.

Lord, let your love shine through my thoughts and words, so 'do not be afraid' is heard as a comfort and not an impossible command.

Seeds of hope

Do not be anxious about anything, but in every situation, by prayer and petition, with thanksgiving, present your requests to God. And the peace of God, which transcends all understanding, will guard your hearts and your minds in Christ Jesus.

When something is worrying you, do you make a note in case you forget it? No, me neither. Usually, I find the opposite is true. Unless I focus on other things, whatever I'm anxious about consumes my thoughts, becoming a fog, obscuring everything else.

Worry is distracting, but if you're like me, being told not to worry isn't going to help. It's like asking someone not to think of a purple elephant. The apostle Paul understands this, recognising that for us to worry less we must consciously think of something else. He suggests focusing on being thankful, acknowledging God's presence in every situation. Staying open to where God is working in our lives prevents us from slipping into feeling that our problems are how life will always be.

We all recognise these types of thoughts: I'll never get well; I'll never find a job; I'll never get out of debt; I'll never kick this addiction; I'll never get married; I'll never make friends; I'll never be able to afford my own home; I'll never lose weight… the list goes on. If I find myself slipping into this way of thinking, I keep a list of good things that happen, however small, and thank God for them at the end of the day. Sometimes I reread what I've written months later, and it helps me see my life in greater perspective: I know when I went through a difficult time, but I also see pages of small kindnesses that I easily could have overlooked. They shine like seeds of hope: a reminder that, whatever our circumstances, God's light is always with us.

Lord, help me to recognise all the good you are working in my life. Amid life's chaos, fill my heart with your peace.

LUKE 2:46, 48

Only human

After three days they found him in the temple courts... His mother said to him, 'Son, why have you treated us like this? Your father and I have been anxiously searching for you.'

Mary and Joseph were observant Jews and travelled every year to Jerusalem for the Passover festival. They went with family and friends, and everything about the celebration was familiar. When Jesus first went missing, they didn't think too much about it – they were travelling and assumed he was with others in the group. It was a day later, when Mary and Joseph asked family and friends where Jesus was, that they realised he wasn't with them. It's every parent's worst nightmare. Telling someone not to be anxious at a time like this is not going to cut it.

It took a day to return to Jerusalem and another three searching the city until Mary and Joseph eventually found Jesus sitting among the teachers in the temple. He was twelve years old – an age when children are striving for independence and parents are all too aware of children's vulnerability. Mary and Joseph were beside themselves with worry and, if we put ourselves in their shoes, we realise this is the most human of emotions.

Sometimes as Christians we think our faith should give us supernatural immunity to anxiety and are disheartened to find it doesn't. Instead of praying for God to strengthen us, we worry about being worried, as if being anxious means our faith isn't strong enough.

Even Mary and Joseph were not immune to anxiety. Being anxious doesn't mean you've lost your faith; it means you're human and you don't have all the answers. Rather than fight this uncomfortable emotion, learn to trust God by accepting how you feel, letting go of control and asking for his help.

Lord, I feel anxious. Please guide me to do what I can to solve my situation and to trust you to deal with that over which I have no control.

Break the habit

'Can any one of you by worrying add a single hour to your life?'

To stop worrying is easier said than done. We can read 'do not worry' in the Bible and feel we're doing something wrong by being anxious, or we can give ourselves a break and recognise that Jesus knows most people, at one time or another, are going to worry. If it was easy to stop, he wouldn't have needed to preach about it so often.

Jesus takes our worries seriously and gives us practical ways to help. He's not an unsympathetic bystander telling us to think positively and just stop worrying. Rather, Jesus helps us to recognise that controlling worry is something we must do consciously and takes effort.

In the past I never gave much thought to worrying. I didn't see it as something within my control. I'd become so used to worrying that it felt part of my personality. It was who I was – I was a worrier. Of course, it's only natural to feel worried when faced with life-changing situations, but many of us live at that heightened level of anxiety all the time. That was how I'd become.

Looking back, I thought I was doing something constructive by worrying. I thought it made me caring and responsible. I was trying to sort things out, foresee problems and prevent them. I now realise I've missed chances to enjoy some wonderful experiences by having my mind caught up in worry about why something happened the way it did, why someone said or did something they did, or about something that might or might not happen in the future.

Worry is tiring, and it's also a habit. Breaking any habit takes time. Jesus invites us to take the first step, recognise worry for what it is and trust him.

Lord, I find myself worrying about many things. Please give me the strength to break this habit and trust you.

JOHN 21:21–22

Other people's business

When Peter saw him, he asked, 'Lord, what about him?' Jesus answered, 'If I want him to remain alive until I return, what is that to you? You must follow me.'

Shortly after his resurrection, Jesus asks Peter for a commitment of love, then says, 'Feed my sheep.' It's a unique calling for Peter to look after the flock, that is, the church. Jesus then says, 'Follow me,' at which point Peter turns and looks towards John, one of the other disciples, and asks, 'Lord, what about him?'

In the last 2,000 years, human nature hasn't changed. I'm sure we've all been like Peter at some point, worrying about what someone else is doing or not doing. When you are a caring person it's easy to get tangled up in other people's problems and messy circumstances. If only he or she would drink less, work harder, take more interest in their children, go to church, take more exercise, quit smoking, lose weight, stop dating that person, look after themselves better, spend more time at home, go out more, be more sociable, talk less, talk more... the list goes on.

When people are close to us, it's difficult to see that other people's problems are not our own and that their responsibilities are not our responsibilities. We can offer advice, provide support and act as an example, but people have the right to make their own choices and learn from their own mistakes, as difficult as that might be to watch. Unless we resist the urge to meddle in other people's business, we can waste significant time and emotional energy trying to 'fix' people, and become distracted from God's call on our lives.

Lord, you have given me the freedom to make my own choices; help me to respect that others have that same freedom, and place in your hands problems that are not mine to interfere in.

In the same boat

No temptation has overtaken you except what is common to mankind. And God is faithful; he will not let you be tempted beyond what you can bear. But when you are tempted, he will also provide a way out so that you can endure it.

When anxious or afraid, it's common to imagine you're the only one to feel this way. This feeling can lead you to keep troubles to yourself, and prevent you from reaching out for support.

When Patricia's spending spiralled out of control, her first reaction was to pretend it wasn't happening. At first, she stopped opening her mail, in case it was a bill she couldn't pay. Shortly after, she stopped opening her door or answering the telephone, in case it was somebody asking for money. Then she became afraid to leave her house, walking her dog at unsociable hours when she thought she'd be least likely to bump into someone.

In desperation, Patricia rang Christians Against Poverty (CAP). 'I didn't hold out much hope for a response,' she says. 'But I knew deep down I needed help, although what help and how that help would come, I didn't know.'

CAP helped Patricia plan a budget and start repaying her debt. CAP also encouraged her to start socialising again, introducing her to people who empathised with her situation. 'There was something comforting about being with other people who were in the same boat,' she says. 'I didn't feel so alone. We were all from different walks of life, but we all had one thing in common – we all had money worries.'

The apostle Paul reminds us that whatever our struggles, we are not alone. Like Patricia, we won't always know when and how help might come, but keeping our heart open to all possibilities will help us recognise and accept it when it does.

Lord, help me remember I don't need to struggle on alone. Keep my heart open to those around me, so I'm able to accept help, wherever it appears.

Trust God

Cast your cares on the Lord and he will sustain you...

Sometimes, we learn to lean on God by practising letting go of small everyday anxieties. At other times, it takes a situation so clearly out of our control – when we have nowhere else to turn but God – before we truly experience what it means to put our trust in him.

Whenever I'm feeling at a loss about what to do, I read Reinhold Niebuhr's 'Serenity prayer' and let the words sink into my heart:

> God, grant me the serenity to accept the things I cannot change, the courage to change the things I can, and the wisdom to know the difference.

There are circumstances beyond our control and questions that will never be answered, no matter how many times we chew them over. Trusting God means we don't need to speculate or overanalyse. If we can do something to help the situation, God will guide us in that direction; no amount of worrying is going to change it.

In my garden, I put smooth pebbles on the top of my plant pots. They look pretty and help protect plants from losing water in the summer months. When I begin to worry about something I'll hold a pebble in my hand, pray about the situation and then lay the pebble down. It feels like releasing a weight and letting go of my illusions of control.

Whenever my thoughts drift back to the same problem, I look out at the garden and feel reassured that God is taking care of it, and then I focus on something else. I might not understand or like where I am, but I feel more peaceful about my lack of control, trusting God will sustain me and work out all things for good.

Lord, guide me to focus my energy on what I can do, and to trust you to deal with matters beyond my control.

Why?

As he went along, he saw a man blind from birth. His disciples asked him, 'Rabbi, who sinned, this man or his parents, that he was born blind?' 'Neither this man nor his parents sinned,' said Jesus, 'but this happened so that the works of God might be displayed in him.'

It's good to ask questions. It's how we learn and grow. Often, our questions lead to more questions as we realise that the more we know the more there is to know. This type of healthy questioning keeps our hearts open with hope to an infinite number of possibilities.

The disciples' question, however, shows how, in grasping for answers, we can close ourselves off from new perspectives. Here, they've already decided someone is to blame for this man's blindness – it's caused either by his sin or the sin of his parents.

When things go wrong, often we want clear answers, reasons why, an explanation, someone to blame. How can a God who is good let such things happen? Jesus' answer provides a whole new perspective, leaving no room for blame, guilt or condemnation. This man's blindness is an instrument through which God's work is made visible. Even today, Jesus' response forces us to question our often narrow view of the world.

How might our vision change if, instead of insisting on a definitive answer for why things happen the way they do, we opened our eyes to the infinite ways God is working in the world? We start by acknowledging God's Spirit, his beauty and his love in each person; choosing hope by keeping our hearts and minds open to 'the other' – whoever or whatever that may be; asking questions to seek harmony not division; and expanding our capacity to love.

Lord, help me not rush to judge and reach for answers I do not have. Guide me to growth through a questioning spirit, and open my heart to the wonder of your works.

Take risks to grow

'Then the man who received one bag of gold came. "Master," he said, "I knew that you are a hard man, harvesting where you have not sown and gathering where you have not scattered seed. So I was afraid and went out and hid your gold in the ground."'

On hearing the parable of the talents there is something disquieting about the master's reaction to the servant who is given only one talent/bag of gold. Depriving the servant of what little he has and giving it to the one who has the most seems inherently unfair.

We can understand the poor servant's caution. It was okay for the other servants with more gold to take a risk, but what if he used his one bag and lost it?

So it is with life. What might seem a small risk to some – like contributing to a class discussion or staff meeting, extending an invitation or trying something new – can feel like an overwhelming challenge to others.

When feeling fragile and anxious we are less likely to participate in life, but the more we get involved with people and activities the more our metaphorical stack of gold begins to grow. Michael Jordan, one of the best basketball players in the sport's history, put it this way: 'I've missed more than 9,000 shots in my career. I've lost almost 300 games. Twenty-six times, I've been trusted to take the game winning shot and missed. I've failed over and over and over again in my life. And that is why I succeed.'

Have you buried your talents in any way? Are there areas in your life where you're holding back because you are afraid you have little to offer or afraid you might fail?

Lord, give me the confidence to participate fully in life and to make the most of the gifts and talents with which you have blessed me.

Grounded in love

Jesus Christ is the same yesterday and today and forever.

We all know change is the only constant in life, but sometimes the speed or scale of change can appear more of a threat than life's natural flow.

Research has shown intolerance of uncertainty is a central element in worry and anxiety. None of us knows for sure what the future will bring, yet when we become anxious we can create a sense of urgency about not knowing. I've been in this situation, where not knowing becomes so stressful I've rushed into decisions I didn't need to make. I've also avoided changes that could have been to my advantage because it felt safer to stay with what I knew.

We all recognise when we're behaving this way – doing anything we can to create certainty – because something about it feels uncomfortable and forced. Demanding an immediate answer rarely leads to the answer we seek. Often it only leads to more unanswered questions and insecurity.

Faith will not rid us of life's problems, but it can help us gain perspective and remain calm amid them. A focus on Jesus reminds us of what we do know – we know that God is good, God is just and God is loving. Nothing and no one can separate us from God. When we allow ourselves to accept this, deep within our being, it frees us to live in hope.

Hope is sometimes presented as wishful thinking, something passive and unrealistic. Hebrews 6:19 talks of hope as being a sure and steadfast 'anchor for the soul'. This image of hope is active and strong. Hope keeps us focused on what is important in life, and prevents us from being swept into a sea of fear and insecurity, by keeping us close to God and grounded in love.

Lord, when all around me feels uncertain, keep my focus on you. Strengthen me with your love, so that I may face the future with an open and fearless heart.

Facing giants

'The Lord who rescued me from the paw of the lion and the paw of the bear will rescue me from the hand of this Philistine.'

There's an old maths joke about a statistics professor who takes a bomb to the airport. When caught, the professor explains, 'I'm reducing my risk of a terrorist attack. I've worked out that the probability of one bomb being on my plane is one in a thousand, but the chance of there being two bombs is one in a million.'

Worry can be a bit like this. It leads us to gather all kinds of evidence to evaluate risk. Often that evidence is negative, turning into an enormous risk assessment as we think about everything that could go wrong and what we might do to prevent it. We've been led to believe that preparing for the worst is realistic and hoping for the best is unrealistic, so we rarely consider what could go in our favour.

When King Saul hears there's a man willing to face the wrath of Goliath he sends for him, only to be dismayed. 'You are not able to go out against this Philistine and fight him; you are only a young man, and he has been a warrior from his youth' (1 Samuel 17:33). But David doesn't see either himself or Goliath the way everyone else does. Instead of focusing on the strength and experience of his opponent, David chooses to focus on his own attributes and draws on his previous successes to give him hope. He recalls how God gave him the strength in the past to fight off lions and bears that were attacking his sheep, and he fires a shot from his sling, just as he'd done many times before, killing the giant with a single blow.

Are you going to be like David and concentrate on what's in your favour? Or, like the other Israelites, are you going to focus on the size and strength of your giants, and why you'll never succeed?

Lord, give me the courage to face my giants by keeping my hope open to all possibilities.

Why not?

For God did not send his Son into the world to condemn the world, but to save the world through him.

In the 1980s I visited Bonn on a school exchange. At the time it was the capital of West Germany, and the Berlin Wall still divided the country. I remember afternoons cycling with my German friend while she spoke passionately, as idealistic young people do, about when, not if, the wall would come down. I had never known Germany without the wall and neither had she. When I got home I said, 'In Germany, they think the wall is coming down.' Of course, I didn't know that. All I knew was what a twelve-year-old girl had told me, but to me at the time hers was the view of the country.

My visit was before Ronald Reagan's famous speech at the Brandenburg Gate in 1987, where the US president urged Mikhail Gorbachev, then General Secretary of the Communist Party of the Soviet Union, to 'tear down this wall!' The wall fell almost two-and-a-half years later, in November 1989, and in October 1990 East and West Germany were reunited after 45 years.

Almost 30 years after the end of the cold war there is still fighting, injustice and persecution across the globe. Reading the news, I sometimes find myself saying, 'The world's gone mad,' or 'What is the world coming to?' or 'It wasn't like this when...'

It's easy to condemn the world, but so much harder to play a part in bringing God's kingdom to earth. I think about my German friend, who didn't have a personal or political influence in bringing down the Berlin Wall. She could have condemned the world, but instead she spoke with hope that the division would end.

Lord, sometimes I feel disheartened by the division and conflict around me. Help me to speak positively of the world and keep my heart open to change for the better.

Rainbow in the clouds

And God said, 'This is the sign of the covenant I am making between me and you and every living creature with you, a covenant for all generations to come: I have set my rainbow in the clouds, and it will be the sign of the covenant between me and the earth.'

During World War II, Ray Rossiter was captured by the Japanese army in Singapore and held as a prisoner of war for three-and-a-half years. Like Eric Lomax, whose story was told in the film *The Railway Man*, Ray survived the building of the Burma railway, known as 'the railway of death' because it claimed 393 lives for every mile of track laid.

I asked Ray how he managed to keep his faith in the face of such deprivation and brutality. He said: 'I felt God was there all the time, his love shining through the actions of men, one for another. He was there in every kindness, every act of compassion – it is how we survived. It was often said, "It is every man for himself in here," but nothing was further from the truth. We depended so much on one another for encouragement, morale boosting and in numerous instances for our very survival.'

Ray's words made me think about how many small acts of kindness we take for granted every day. We can easily overlook the significance of small gestures in enriching our lives. Yet in those prisoner-of-war camps, when every dignity was stripped away, it was these same small kindnesses that kept hope alive. They shone, like the brilliance of a rainbow in the rain.

Lord, when the rains of life come, let me feel the warmth of your love shine on me like the sun, so that among the clouds I also see the colour and beauty of life.

All creation

'For in him we live and move and have our being.'

The wonderful complexity and mystery of life cannot be captured in words, yet we need some way of expressing how we move along the journey. In her book *Wait and Trust*, Angela Ashwin gives us a beautiful image: 'When we try to find God by anxiously searching we are like fish swimming round and round, furiously hunting for the ocean.' In other words, while at times we can be more aware of his presence all around us, whatever happens we can never be separated from God.

It's a reassuring image and a unifying one. He is God of all creation. We are not isolated beings; we are part of something much bigger. In giving us free will, God has done what all great leaders do: he's not dictated how life will be; he's invited us to share with him in the ongoing creation of the world.

When feeling anxious it can be difficult to see outside of ourselves and our fears. It's often said that by taking the focus off our worries and helping others we begin to help ourselves. When I find myself worrying about division and destruction in the world today, I remind myself of the wisdom of St Teresa of Avila, who said, 'Christ has no body now on earth but yours. No hands but yours, no feet but yours. Yours are the hands by which he is to bless us now.'

We can worry about the lack of care we see in the world, but community doesn't just happen; it is something we need to play our part to achieve. Here lies the challenge, because it requires more than money – it demands a change of heart. It demands we recognise we are all connected, swimming in the ocean of God's grace.

Lord, help me recognise your grace flowing all around me, so that I feel safe removing any emotional barriers I've built between myself and others.

Another way

I remain confident of this: I will see the goodness of the Lord in the land of the living. Wait for the Lord; be strong and take heart and wait for the Lord.

At the closing ceremony of the inaugural Invictus Games in London, Prince Harry read an email from a woman called Kara who had been living with autoimmune problems for ten years: 'Up until my awareness of the Invictus Games, I was living in memories and mourning for what I had lost when I got sick at the age of 24. In my mind, my life was over and I was just waiting to be done, because I felt I wasn't capable of doing or living like I used to. I'm starting to think now that my game has just begun too.'

Sometimes it feels like life is all about waiting – waiting in line; waiting for exam results; waiting for the response to a job application; waiting for medical test results; waiting for treatment; or waiting to feel differently. There are also times, like for Kara, when something life-changing happens and it's difficult to imagine how life can ever be good again.

Often, viewing a situation another way can be the first step to restoring hope. Waiting can feel passive and helpless. It can also leave us static, unable to see a way forward. What are we meant to do while we wait? Today's psalm shows us how to wait actively, with confidence, optimism and strength of heart.

Knowing we will see God's goodness in this world creates an attitude of anticipation rather than dread. When we stop putting limits on God, we recognise his healing works in infinite ways and our hearts become open to help wherever and from whoever it appears. In this sense, waiting for God becomes freeing rather than restrictive. It allows us to live fully, focusing on what we can do, trusting God to guide our next steps when we're ready to make them, and inspiring others along the way.

Lord, I am hurting. Strengthen me with patience and awaken my hope, to trust you can work goodness in any situation.

Love

...the earth is full of his unfailing love.

Every day there are new stories about terrible things happening in the world. Today I opened the newspaper to see a story about a four-year-old girl who was duct-taped to a chair while at her nursery, by staff who then posted her picture on social media. The evidence was there for everyone to see, a frightened child staring into the camera lens, firmly taped twice around her body to a plastic chair.

Who would do such a thing? Is this a world full of unfailing love? This incident happened in Missouri, halfway across the world from me. Of course, that doesn't make it any less upsetting for those involved, but I remind myself it's unusual for nursery staff to behave this way. If this happened every day it wouldn't be news.

It's the same with news of paedophile clergy or corrupt police officers. If their actions weren't considered out of the ordinary, they wouldn't be news. It's when these acts stop being news that we should really start to worry. Yet, because we get 24-hour news from across the globe, these shocking occurrences can feel commonplace.

When we start to feel this way, it's good to remind ourselves of the kindnesses that surround us every day and never make the headlines. Fred Rogers, the American TV personality and Presbyterian minister, used to tell a story about being reassured as a child whenever the news scared him:

> My mother would say to me, 'Look for the helpers. You will always find people who are helping.' To this day, especially in times of 'disaster', I remember my mother's words and I am always comforted by realising that there are still so many helpers – so many caring people in the world.

Is there any kindness in your life that's become so common you take it for granted?

Lord, help me recognise the opportunities to love in everything I do, and open my eyes to the beauty, joy and wonder of your world.